W9-BCC-911

Running Rats

Kelly Doudna
AUTHOR

C. A. Nobens
ILLUSTRATOR

Consulting Editor, Diane Craig, M.A./Reading Specialist

ABDO
Publishing Company

Published by ABDO Publishing Company, 4940 Viking Drive, Edina, Minnesota 55435.

CREDITS

Edited by: Pam Price

Concept Development: Nancy Tuminelly

Cover and Interior Design and Production: Mighty Media

Photo Credits: Corbis Images, GK Hart/Vikki Hart/Getty Images, Klein & Hubert/BIOS/Peter Arnold, Inc., Labat & Rouquette/PHONE/BIOS/Peter Arnold, Inc., ShutterStock

LIBRARY OF CONGRESS CATALOGING-IN-PUBLICATION DATA

Doudna, Kelly, 1963-
  Running rats / Kelly Doudna ; illustrated by C.A. Nobens.
    p. cm. -- (Perfect pets)
  ISBN-13: 978-1-59928-754-6
  ISBN-10: 1-59928-754-4
  1. Rats as pets--Juvenile literature. I. Nobens, C. A., ill. II. Title.

  SF459.R3D68 2007
  636.9'352--dc22
                                          2006033255

SandCastle™ books are created by a professional team of educators, reading specialists, and content developers around five essential components—phonemic awareness, phonics, vocabulary, text comprehension, and fluency—to assist young readers as they develop reading skills and strategies and increase their general knowledge. All books are written, reviewed, and leveled for guided reading, early reading intervention, and Accelerated Reader® programs for use in shared, guided, and independent reading and writing activities to support a balanced approach to literacy instruction.

SandCastle Level: Transitional

LET US KNOW

SandCastle would like to hear your stories about reading this book. What is your favorite page? Was there something hard that you needed help with? Share the ups and downs of learning to read. We want to hear from you! To get posted on the ABDO Publishing Company Web site, send us e-mail at:

sandcastle@abdopublishing.com

RATS

Rats are smart, social animals. They like to run around, but they can also be calm and cuddly at times.

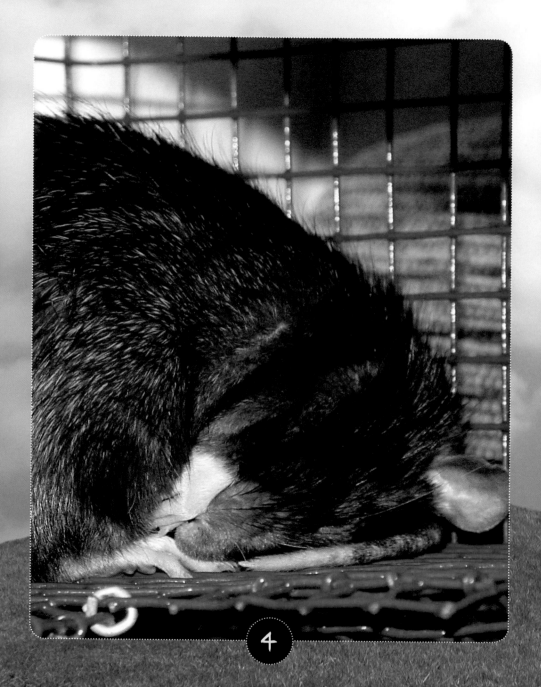

Cody's rat is taking a nap in its cage. Cody cleans the cage every week.

Andrea has an exercise wheel for her rat to run in. The wheel is fun for her rat and helps him stay fit.

7

Richard gives his rats food and fresh water every day. Cherries are a favorite treat!

Patrick takes his rat to the veterinarian for a checkup. The vet listens to the rat's breathing.

Kimberly and Kylie play with their rats. Rats need attention and playtime outside of their cages.

A Rat Story

Matt's friend Fred
is a big black rat.
Fred likes to play in
Matt's cowboy hat.

16

Matt puts the cowboy
hat right over Fred.
Fred sticks out his nose
and then his whole head.

Fred runs up Matt's arm
and makes a soft squeak.
Fred twitches his whiskers
and tickles Matt's cheek.

19

Matt scratches Fred's head between his round ears. Matt says, "I hope you live for a hundred years!"

Fun facts

Rats use their tails to regulate their body temperature, to communicate with each other, and to balance when they climb.

Rats can swim, and they can breathe underwater for up to two minutes.

A rat can chew through concrete.

Ancient Romans considered rats to be good luck.

Rats regularly clean and groom themselves.

Glossary

attention – the act of concentrating on or giving careful thought to something.

calm – quiet and peaceful.

checkup – a routine examination by a doctor.

cuddly – suitable for being held close.

favorite – someone or something that you like best.

fit – healthy and in good physical shape.

treat – something special.

veterinarian – a doctor who takes care of animals.

About SandCastle™

A professional team of educators, reading specialists, and content developers created the SandCastle™ series to support young readers as they develop reading skills and strategies and increase their general knowledge. The SandCastle™ series has four levels that correspond to early literacy development in young children. The levels are provided to help teachers and parents select appropriate books for young readers.

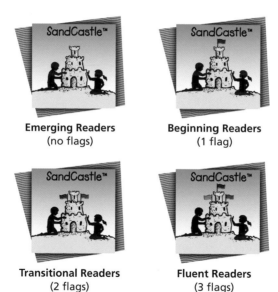

Emerging Readers
(no flags)

Beginning Readers
(1 flag)

Transitional Readers
(2 flags)

Fluent Readers
(3 flags)

These levels are meant only as a guide. All levels are subject to change.

To see a complete list of SandCastle™ books and other nonfiction titles from ABDO Publishing Company, visit **www.abdopublishing.com** or contact us at: 4940 Viking Drive, Edina, Minnesota 55435 • 1-800-800-1312 • fax: 1-952-831-1632